POCHSY IV
UNPLUGGED

POCHSY IV
UNPLUGGED

KAREN HINES

FOREWORD BY
BRUCE MCCULLOCH

INTRODUCTION BY
KATHLEEN OLIVER

COACH HOUSE BOOKS, TORONTO

first edition

Canada Council for the Arts Conseil des Arts du Canada

Canada

ONTARIO ARTS COUNCIL
CONSEIL DES ARTS DE L'ONTARIO
an Ontario government agency
un organisme du gouvernement de l'Ontario

Published with the generous assistance of the Canada Council for the Arts and the Ontario Arts Council. Coach House Books also acknowledges the support of the Government of Canada through the Canada Book Fund and the Government of Ontario through the Ontario Book Publishing Tax Credit.

LIBRARY AND ARCHIVES CANADA CATALOGUING IN PUBLICATION

Title: Pochsy. IV, Unplugged / Karen Hines ; foreword by Bruce McCulloch ; introduction by Kathleen Oliver.
Names: Hines, Karen, author | McCulloch, Bruce, writer of foreword | Oliver, Kathleen, 1964- writer of introduction
Description: First edition.
Identifiers: Canadiana (print) 20250120976 | Canadiana (ebook) 20250121131 | ISBN 9781552454954 (softcover) | ISBN 9781770568518 (EPUB) | ISBN 9781770568631 (PDF)
Subjects: LCGFT: Drama.
Classification: LCC PS8615.I44 P625 2025 | DDC C812/.6—dc23

Pochsy IV: Unplugged is available as an ebook: ISBN 978 1 77056 851 8 (EPUB), ISBN 978 1 77056 863 1 (PDF)

Purchase of the print version of this book entitles you to a free digital copy. To claim your ebook of this title, please email sales@chbooks.com with proof of purchase. (Coach House Books reserves the right to terminate the free digital download offer at any time.)

For Margot

'Bouffons are the hunchbacks, the lepers, the syphilitics; everything society has rejected. But they come to tell us, God's beautiful children, that all aspects of humanity belong to everyone. In the grotesqueness of the bouffon is a truth about humanity.'

– Philippe Gaulier

'What we need is a clown for our times. A clown that gives us a larger sense of God in each of us, that celebrates our humanness, our animalness, and the times we can touch each other in a moment of laughter.' – Richard Pochinko

FOREWORD

BRUCE MCCULLOCH

When Karen asked me to write the foreword for *Pochsy IV: Unplugged*, I thought two things: 'Wow, what an honour!' and 'Damn, she's figured out a way to get me to read it again.' Don't get me wrong: this is a hilarious and brilliant play. But there were times along the way when she needed a bit of encouragement. Easy. As a lifelong friend and a fan, I loved reading and rereading as she shaped this amazing piece.

The writer, like the performer, is obsessive and caring. She can rewrite a stage direction forty times. That's why, in the end, everything is so evocative, rich, and efficient. I could reread her stage directions all day. But what's *in* the play is even better; it is not a scream but a purr in the face of the oncoming darkness.

Pochsy walks out on stage both fierce and vulnerable. She only has her red lipstick, her tiny leather punk teddy-bear backpack, and her wit to protect her. To protect *us*, from the onslaught of the 'endless deprivation of this worldly experience.'

Pochsy sings, flirts, and roams the stage like a curious and brooding stand-up who keeps asking herself, 'How am I doing?' Well, really, how *can* she be doing? How can *anyone* be doing in these dark and surreal times? She hovers above the proceedings like a high-wire artist who almost slips but *never* falls. You're terrified, but instinctively you know you're in capable hands. In the hands of someone who understands that this world is both horrifying and beautiful.

As a comic, I think what we don't say enough about Karen's work is that it's hilarious. Classic jokes are often mumbled or thrown away like a master. A master who tries to disguise her mastery, which makes it all the more effective. Her meditations on 'us' and on the world are remarkable. We trust her, even if sometimes her attention seems misplaced – she's more worried about mislabelling bird parts than she is about picking mercury up off the floor with her bare fingers.

As a writer, Karen is both fierce and kitten-ear soft. Her work is biting satire, but with a warm and loving heart. We may be wondering, can we make it through this savage, hilarious time? She points out that we already have. Because she has at last set down this tiny, incredible work, and we're all here to share it.

INTRODUCTION

KATHLEEN OLIVER, PLAYWRIGHT AND THEATRE CRITIC

We live in a scary time. Even scarier than when Pochsy first made her entrance into the world and changed my life.

September 1992. *Pochsy's Lips* had been touring fringe festivals all summer, and by the time it arrived in Vancouver, the last stop on the circuit, the buzz had built to the point where it was *the* show to see: all over town, Pochsy's waifish, sepulchral face gazed out from the cover of the *Georgia Straight*, Vancouver's arts weekly.

In the long-vanished Hot Jazz Club on Main Street, I was enthralled. A tiny woman in baby-doll pyjamas tells us she's dying (it probably has something to do with her job at Mercury Packers, where she packs mercury), while spouting advertising jingles and singing cheerful little songs. Perched demurely on the razor's edge of humour and horror, Pochsy (an anagram of *psycho*, but also toxic, as in the pox, but also kind of cute because of that *y* at the end) is an unapologetic narcissist, delusional, dangerous, flirtatious, mean ... and so *adorable*! I watched the whole show open-mouthed.

At a time when anything dark or transgressive was lazily dubbed 'satire,' though it often wasn't clear what exactly was being satirized, Pochsy's targets – consumer culture and its disastrous effects on our humanity and the world we live in – were unmistakable. And they hurt. We could laugh at the extremity of her behaviour, but then catch ourselves in our complicity. Almost every laugh had a catch like that.

Sometimes the most powerful moments in satire are when an unreliable character speaks the exact truth. When, near the end of *Pochsy's Lips*, she says, 'We live at a time when imagining a meaningful future is irrational and unrealistic,' there is no irony. Still, she chooses to be hopeful.

And who could have imagined the future Pochsy has ended up having? *Oh, Baby* and *Citizen Pochsy*, both prequels to the first play, fed the hunger for this irresistible character in the decade that followed. Karen continued to develop her deliciously unique sensibility and style in her dazzling multi-character plays and brilliant personal essays. While nothing can compare to seeing these shows live, there's an added dimension to the experience of reading them: the precise diction in her meticulous stage directions is a delight.

When Karen told me she was working on *Pochsy IV*, I was thrilled. While their trappings may have changed a bit – yesterday's affirmations are today's psychotropic microdoses – Pochsy's satiric targets have only grown in scale and urgency, and it's harder than ever to be hopeful. Metastatic capitalism and its collateral damage hit home in this play when Mercury Packers outsources its operations and Pochsy loses her job. She is more on the precipice than ever. Her love-hate relationship with the audience has intensified. She recognizes the corporate gaslighting in her layoff letter, but she still unboxes fetishistically. Sound familiar?

Pochsy recognizes her powerlessness, but she's also powerless to change. That doesn't stop her from continuing to contemplate meeeaning. And inviting you into her dreams. I think you should go join her there now; it's a trip you may never fully return from.

For someone who's been dying since the moment she was born (but aren't we all?), Pochsy has had a remarkably long life. May it never end.

PLAYWRIGHT'S NOTE
(WITH FILES FROM *THE POCHSY PLAYS*)

In my twenties, I designed Pochsy as a microcosm. An avatar torn from the ragged edges of capitalism, trailing the destruction of consumer obsessions at the same time as she is excited by them. Ultimately alone, perpetually lost. By the way, I just looked up 'lost,' seeking a synonym, but all I got was the TV series *Lost*. Pochsy would be thrilled. Pochsy is God-fearing, but also God-flirty – and ultimately condescending. She sees right through him. Sorry: Him.

This is the fourth in the Pochsy series. It was written after a nearly two-decade break since the last. It was written on a dare. My friend Bruce, who wrote this book's foreword, said one day during the early days of lockdown, 'Irony is dead.' He seemed to be beseeching me to right that wrong. With Pochsy. Turns out he was messing with me. It was a cruel joke.

I, along with many others who write satire, became paralyzed in that moment, when dark comedy seemed to have lost Death as its ace comedic tool. It was only when I turned to my creation and the mercury-laced coils of her seemingly unbalanced mind that I found a way through – when I asked myself, 'What Would Pochsy Do?'

Pochsy onstage borrows from a kind of alchemy: a tactical blend of clowning and bouffon as those distinct styles were taught to me by master teachers Richard Pochinko and Philippe Gaulier. The performance first thrived under Sandra Balcovske, who had mentored and directed me at Toronto's

Second City and then directed the first two Pochsy plays. I also called on my academic studies in Taoist philosophy and film theory and a course on Luis Buñuel. And some beginner singing lessons and ballet classes of childhood.

WWPD? Anything to entertain, while I stand off to the side, trying to figure shit out.

My collaborator John Turner (director of the third *Pochsy* show and credited in this book as 'Clunic Consultant') tells his clown students that bouffons are 'the special forces' of clown. That where clowns must love their audience, bouffons must *use* love to make their kills. Their moves must be surgical if they are to get away with their deadly subversions. But in 2021, as a basically fortunate Canadian, what could I target in *Pochsy IV*? How could I possibly 'kill' the tender people in the room who were already going through so much, or criticize what felt like an already-wrecked world? Who was I to hold a mirror up to a scarily fragmented society?

'Irony depends upon interpretation; it "happens" in the tricky, unpredictable space between expression and understanding,' writes Linda Hutcheon in *Irony's Edge: The Theory and Politics of Irony*.

WWPD? Find that tricky space and make it her *chaise*.

Pochsy never forgets she's doing a show. She will notice lighting shifts, or perhaps seem to will them to happen. Perhaps the most important thing to know about the performance style is the direct contact between Pochsy and the audience. She sees and hears the audience. She looks into their eyes. She may bless a sneezing audience member. If a phone rings, she may invite the owner to answer, and will patiently hold the show until they're done. As in any public intervention, the venom must be delivered with finesse. Charm lets her get away with murder.

Pochsy has always been at home sliding across spectrums. Sashaying between cruelty and sweetness, victim and manipulator, blasphemy and reverence. Pochsy *deploys* all these opposites to entertain, or surprise, or make the audience laugh in the name of a bigger game. And in the end, Pochsy's success depends on her capacity to include the playwright as a target.

The first Pochsy play was set in a hospital room. The second on a beautiful but toxic beach made of slag. The third in the waiting room for a deadly audit. They can be seen or read in any order. I see *Pochsy IV* as living, in clown-logic chronology, between the first and second plays. Or just before the first. It truly doesn't matter. In the end, these narratives are just files holding systems of satire that allow me to expose and examine my deepest fears and obsessions.

NB: Stage directions are very detailed in this book. They are not meant as prescriptive, but rather as a record of what has occurred on stage. Or, in a few cases, they denote new bits in the works. (This book is going to press just as we go into rehearsal for *Pochsy IV*'s Toronto premiere in April 2025. There is a lot happening in the world, and there are bound to be little changes.)

Karen Hines, March 2025

Production Notes

Place: Industrial. Abandoned. Corrugated iron and painted brick. There is vapour in the air.

Lights: Industrial/Concert. There are moving spotlights like on a packing floor, only these ones are smooth, like theatre lights. They will follow Pochsy attentively.

Set: Almost nothing. Although there is a white chaise to the side somewhere – a cross between a designer lawn chair and a medical cot. There is also a pile of what seem like old first-aid kits nearby.

Props: On the white chaise, there is a miniature black knapsack. The knapsack is a teddy bear made of black leather, zippers, and safety pins. Rivets. It is cute but also not cute.

Sound: At centre stage, there is a microphone on a stand. Old-school: tight metal grille over the mic's capsule. The mic is not cordless: its cord snakes almost excessively around the stage floor.

Pochsy's voice is amplified through the mic. The sound of her voice is always 'surround.'

Some songs are underscored with a phantom steel guitar. Some are not. Throughout the performance, there are almost-subliminal sound pads underscoring scenes, like in the movies – like in thrillers or cartoons.

Pochsy's Costume: Industrial-chic; whimsi-goth; factory-floor-siren; Ghoul Friday. It's a timeless shipping-and-receiving uniform (boots, work dress, and safety elements) but dialled up with glittering details.

Hair and Makeup: Pochsy's long black hair is shiny and nearly impossibly perfect. Face: White Frost. Eyes: Carbon. Lips: Hollywood Red.

Production History

Pochsy IV: Unplugged premiered at the 2023 High Performance Rodeo, where it was presented by One Yellow Rabbit Performance Theatre in Calgary.

Production Credits

Written and performed by Karen Hines
Directed by Michael Kennard
Dramaturgy by Blake Brooker
Lighting and Set Design by Sandi Somers
Music and Sound Design by Chantal Vitalis
Additional Sounds: Richard Feren
Clunic Consultant: John Turner
Costume Consultant: Justin Miller/Pearle Harbour
Graphic Artist: Peter Moller
Photography: Gary Mulcahey
Social Media and Design: Kate Pallesen
Production Associate: Dianne Goodman
Producer: Keep Frozen

Acknowledgements of Support

Pochsy IV: Unplugged was developed through performances from 2021 to 2024 at In the Soil Festival, Theatre Network at the Roxy, Play the Fool Festival, and, originally, in late-night performances at One Yellow Rabbit Performance Theatre. It will have its Toronto premiere at VideoCabaret in 2025.

Pochsy IV was supported through its early development by the Canada Council for the Arts, the Alberta Foundation for the Arts, and the Banff Centre, Leighton Studios.

POCHSY IV: UNPLUGGED

(From blackness.)

(A ghosting of backlight reveals Pochsy in a vaporous cloud. Like a delicate zombie, she steps out. We do not see her face, just the misty outline of her body.)

(In a recording, over a rickety PA, we hear Pochsy's voice, amplified. She sounds like an old radio station trying to come in.)

POCHSY (IN VOICEOVER): Every morning, in the morning, I wake up in the dead of night and I ask myself, 'Who am I?

'Who am I *now* … ?'

(Very gradually, light creeps around Pochsy's body. She appears to be wrapped in a shaggy fur. Over the PA, her voice continues: gritty radio.)

Every morning, in the morning, I polish my teeth with fish-friendly tooth polish and watch the foam swirl down the drain where it will mingle with the foam from a billion other teeth. And I know I am not alone.

Still I wonder …

Who am I now?

(The light comes from all sides now: ghostly, soft. We see that the fur she's wearing is a lush black fur hoodie.)

Every morning, I step into the shower where I wash and repair my *damaged* hair … then I stroke on my false-lash-effect UV-60 mascara to which I am *addicted* and which suits my skin-first minimalistic makeup by which I am *obsessed* …

(She tilts her face up to catch the light.)

Plus, a little kiss-proof lip stain never killed anybody.

(Beat.)

Or, like, anybody human …

(She tips her face back down.)

Every morning, I slide behind the wheel of my Pontiac Impatience, power-lock my crumple-proof doors, and as my fingers trace my complicated touch screen, it asks me:

Where I am going.

Where I am going now.

It tells me:

Follow the blue line.

Follow it now …

(Music pulses. Pochsy approaches the microphone at centre stage. Vapour swirls around her. A ghostly beam of light hits her face: small and soft.)

POCHSY: *(murmuring live now, into the mic)* Good evening. And thank you, everybody, for coming along. On this night. At this time.

For those of you who know me, my name is Pochsy.

For those of you who do not know me, my name is Pochsy.

Taxpayer, working girl.

(Music swells. She sings.)

> The darkness was deep and quiet was soft.
> It was painless on ice, but lonelier than time.
> I gave you my hand and you raised me from under,
> Now I'll be yours, if you'll be mine.

(The ghostly light intensifies, brightening Pochsy's face, and now highlighting her industrial work gloves: nitrile, tight, sea-green. She's gripping the mic stand. She stares directly into the audience's eyes.)

Thank you for making this a great and funnn-tastic occasion. Sort of like a dinner party without the food. Like a birthday party without the birth. A pool party without the lifeguard. But then really, riiight? Lifeguards are such alarmists …

(She sings.)

> The apple is seedless, just take a bite,
> The manna's baked fresh for you tonight.
> God's tears soothe my flesh, SPF 9-9-NEIN.
> God's so great! He says, No, dear, the Glory is thine!

And I'm like, wow, my Lord. Thankyaoooowwww *(Pochsy sustains an absurd but gentle vocal fry).*

(She takes the mic from the stand and takes a step or two toward the people.)

So, I listened to you all, as you were entering just now, in your lightweight transparent plastic-rimmed glasses and your mindfully reconstructed Levi's and your Patagonia save-the-planet vests with their little interior pockets filled with gummies and psilocybin, murmuring to each other about the universal debt and the wicked One Percent … And I just had to pinch myself.

I dreamed you.

I manifesssted you.

I have been moving toward this moment since I was a baby.

(She sings.)

I was born in a nursery with poor ventilation,
I learned how to walk on a neo-foundation,
I booked a dark passage and somehow survived.
Now I've spent all my savings just being alive.

(Light now gets a little more intense: shafts and haze all around. Pochsy gets hotter on the mic, but more sotto voce.)

As you entered tonight, I listened to you because I believe it is important to listen to every person's lived experience – while simultaneously comparing it with my own.

(She strikes a pose, extends her arms gloriously.)

And as I donned my Panda fur – and yes, it is Panda – don't worry, it's recycled – I meant to order knockoff Prada but I'm on and/or am appropriating the 'dyslexia spectrum' and so I wound up with *Panda*, just with the white patches removed, leaving oblivion blue-black as my environmental statement.

(She strokes one furry sleeve like it's a pet.)

And as I packed my own gummies and zipped up my miniature knapsack – because I already have too much to bear – *(the little leather teddy pack on the chaise gets hit with its own mini spotlight)* I was thinking about the time before we all existed, and imagining the time after we all die.

That is, I was pondering the nothingness that bounds either side of my life. *(She remembers the audience.)* Your lives. The fact that all pain ceases, after a time, and the mind-body problem vanishes. And the endless deprivation of this worldly experience gives way to eternity, where supply chains all lead to a place where nothingness isn't 'a thing.'

(Silence. Stillness. Pochsy stares into the void. Then:)

Please sing with me!

(Music swells.)

Doo, doo, doo, doo … Yes, that's right!

(She leads the audience in what is a pretty complicated tune.)

Doo doo doo doo … Yes, yes, and if you are a very good singer, softly …

Doo doo doo … And if you are not a good singer, please feel free not to – don't.

(Music out.)

We don't need everybody.

(Beat.)

I think we never have needed everybody.

Perhaps that has been our problem:

We. Don't. Actually need. Everybody.

Like a mama deer with Fawn A and Fawn B …

(softly) One of them may have to go.

(Music back in. She sings.)

> The darkness is deep and the morning is night,
> I will hold you real close so the bad bugs don't bite,
> And if the bough breaks and the cradle falls free,
> Uh-oh, I'll rock you if you'll rock me.

(She takes her mic off the stand and steps toward the audience.)

As I said to my co-worker the other day, as we stood drinking our post-work coffees in their avant-garde corporate-cafeteria-pink-beet-dyed compostable cups, bathed in the fading light off a literal salt mine, I said:

'I believe that if death is synonymous with the end of experience, so it must be. And it is *(she reaches for the word)* the intraaaansigency of everything that magnifies the beauty.'

For example:

If those salt mines lasted forever, we would grow blind to them. Like the glaciers we can't bear to watch melt – thank you, Greta Thunberg, for ruining my peace, but please, I already have the memory of about a billion rapid tests eating a hole in my mind: a plastic-and-cardboard-shaped hole that will never be filled, except perhaps with a Fossil cross-body bag.

(small interior lurch) And I'm sorry, I don't mean a cross 'body bag.'

I mean a leather bag that straps across the body.

A purse-bag.

With six pockets.

And concealed zippers …

(Awkward beat; she checks to see if the room is digging it.)

But that those glaciers still exist now means the fact of their existence will never end. And that they will exist eternally means that you will never not-cease to not-be *(stumbling)* I'm not sure I got that … part … right … *Dooby, doo-dooby-doo dooby, doom-doom.*

(Over the following, Pochsy reaches out to the audience like a surreal flight attendant, conjuring upcoming delights and pointing to non-existent exits.)

So, take my hand, fall into my eyes,
Walk the water's edge with me.
Above, the purple sky's flooded with doves
And shiny black ducks paddle peacefully.

(very quiet) Yeah, take my hand, fall into my eyes,
The water is glass, the moon's sub-marine.
Fish gotta swim, deer gotta get by,
Still I hope you can feel the love in this dream.

So, thank you all for coming along. My name is Pochsy. And this is my show.

(Musical kill-sting. Flash and Smoke. Blackout.)

(Immediately, lights surge back: Pochsy's ghostly light gives way to a shimmering showbiz spotlight; a Taylor Swiftian helicopter-gods-light of a spot. Pochsy is clearly comfortable in such a light. This light will follow her now, most of the time, for the rest of the show.)

Rider

So… It really is good to be here tonight. With you.

I wasn't actually sure if I was going to be able to make it myself, I dunno, I've just been super-busy, like suuuuper busy, and … I just found it really hard to make the commitment.

'At this time.'

(She takes the mic from its stand, then drapes her arm over the stand stand-up-comedy-style.)

But then I read the liability rider? On the contract? Where it says that …

(She strolls with the mic. Her brilliant follow-spot follows her. She knows the rider by rote.)

'If the performance or any part thereof is prevented or rendered impossible or "not feasible" by any act or regulation, public authority, or bureau, delay in transportation services or interruption thereof, by any strike, fire, civil tumult, epidemic, nuclear strike, or "other warfare," or by "any cause beyond the reasonable control of either party, including but not limited to Acts of God" … neither party will be bound by the terms of this agreement."

(Beat.)

And so I felt much better. Because I felt less obligated. And so I'm here. And so are you. And all I can say is … phew!

(She looks into every person's eyes. Then:)

(Very softly.) Excuse me.

Gummy

(Pochsy sets down the mic and crosses the stage, doffing her panda fur jacket in an alluring way. She lays the fur down in the shadows somewhere.

We now see her work uniform, which looks like something she might have bought in the Magical Realism Industrial Chic Shoppe. The jumper-dress is ankle-length, flowy, but the skirts are layered with rugged, possibly chemical-resistant activated carbon and vapour-protective barrier films. Below it all, heavy, glossy black work boots.

What looks at first like a laced-up corset reveals itself in light to be an industrial-style back brace like those used by many warehouse employees who do heavy lifting. The brace is also glossy and black with many criss-crossing straps. It cinches Pochsy's waist in a flattering way. There are sparkling clasps and rivets. Pochsy's sea-green nitrile gloves pop against it all.)

'Fit check, friends?

(She giggles and poses three ways for the audience, showing off the boots, back brace, and gloves. As she twirls, she flashes the vapour-protective barrier films. Which look like a Black Swan's crinoline.)

(Pochsy goes to the white chaise and lifts up her miniature-knapsack leather teddy bear. She turns the bear over like a baby for burping, then unzips its back and reaches her whole hand into its body. Pulls out a THC *gummy envelope: bright pink. She tries to open it but can't crack the child-proof packaging. Really can't open it. It is impossible to open.)*

Mmf!

(She gives up. Tosses the bear back onto the chaise. Returns to her mic.)

Um … *(she holds up the gummy package)* Is there a child in the house?

(She accidentally cracks the gummy seal.)

Ooh!

(Pops a gummy.)

Don't worry, it's nothing weird. Just a little medicinal. It's for, um …

(Looks down. Reads the label. Looks up.)

'Mild anxiety.'

Which … I don't think anyone actually even *has* that anymore!

(Pochsy performs a brief ASMR *with the gummy envelope, holding it very close to the microphone's grille: soft foil crinkling, plastic zipper-closure closing. More crinkling. It is quite loud.)*

I normally prefer a little molly before the show, but I feared it might mess with my focus. On this night. *(flirtatious)* Falling in love with so many people at one time. *(She falls a bit in love with them.)* Might tangle my narrative …

(She drops the gummy packet onto the floor. Then, unapologetic:)

Oopsydaisy.

(She kicks the packet away.)

Don't worry, though; gummy won't kick in until after the show. So it will not interfere with my intention. Which is to unify this room. To somehow parse that unpredictable space between expression and understanding.

Between what I say and *(coy)* what I will later claim to have said.

(coyer) Or to have *meant* …

(She seems to look into each patron's eyes.)

You're like a mirror, all of you, broken into shards, each with your own psychic algorithms pulsing through your magical veins.

(Pochsy replaces her mic on its stand. She breathes into the mic deeply. Lights get cooler. The bright spot softens a little. There is more vapour in the air.)

Mercury Packers

So … my name is Pochsy and … until very recently, I had a job.

I worked at Mercury Packers. Where I packed mercury.

It was right across the street from my house, which was great for me. Because it just took me a minute. To drive.

(Little pause.)

It was a good job. At a good company. A company built on the twin principles of respect for the individual and a commitment to the ideal.

They say we worked inhuman hours. But then they were set by humans, so, really, they were human hours. But …

(Little pause.)

It was a good job.
Two weeks' vacation every year.

Great cafeteria.

And a relaxed dress code, which allowed me to take my personal identity and my professional identity and make a third thing that was … a third thing.

Plus, it was super-safe. Eventually. Since the filters.

Once the disaaaaster …

(Little pause.)

Unfortunately, I recently received this letter … in the actual mail.

(She pulls out a letter that is tucked into her corset/brace, unfolds it, and weirdly aggressively smacks the paper across the mic: super loud. She reads:)

'Dear Mercury Packers Contractor,'

(to the audience) Which someone struck through and wrote *(fake glee)*, 'POCHSY (exclamation mark, exclamation mark, exclamation mark).'

(She stares at the letter, darkly fixed, then reads:)

'It is with great sadness that Mercury Packers has made the decision to terminate your contract, effective immediately, even as we value the many contributions you have made over the last many years' – *(to the audience)* which they used 'many' twice, just saying …

(She reads.) 'Unfortunately, due to the rising costs of organic chemical elements everywhere, Mercury Packers has been forced to off-shore its operations' *(to the audience)* to, I suppose, the land where inhuman hours are human … because of the time difference … ?

Then *(she skims)* corporate talk, legalese, gaslight-gaslight, incomprehensible severance formula, vapour, vapour, and finally,

'Wishing you nothing …

(Way long pause.)

… but the best.'

'Your friends at Mercury Packers.

'Catalyzing the Ideal Since 1939.'

(Pochsy looks at the letter a long time. Then she crushes it into the mic. Wipes the mic with it. The sound is crazy loud.)

(She drops the crushed letter onto the ground, where it is lit by a very tiny spotlight. The letter will remain lit, glowing there for the rest of the show. Pochsy stares at it for a moment, then:)

Anyway, thanks to globafuckalization I no longer have a job, or let's say a robot has my job. Or perhaps a child.

And I'm sorry, I mean no offence to children. Or robots.

Although at Mercury Packers, the bots did begin to show signs of privilege-mentality … bot biases …

Bot grievances.

ANYWAY, since Mercury Packers, I have been having trouble pivoting. I applied to grad school. Just to buy some time. Went on the university portal. Clicked on 'Neuro Science.' Accidentally. Because I misread it as 'Euro Science'

– which I already have the wardrobe! *(She spins, poses, and gestures toward her resting panda fur.)*

I did not get in, seeing as I have no academic credentials. Seeing as I started working for my company when I was *(venomous)* sixteen.

But it's okay. Because I believe the universe is a powerful force.

(She looks up and out.)

The universe will protect me.

Prayer

(A kaleidoscopic beam shines down upon her, like a multi-coloured chapel light, only trippier.)

Dear Lord,

(Pochsy clasps her hands in prayer.)

Please forgive me for all of the evil and weak things I have done in my life. Please give me the courage and the strength to carry on.

Grant me the faith to dream great dreams, even now, at this 'time,' this time now, regardless of how endless this time may turn out to be.

Forgive me the sin of Vanity, which compels me toward parabens and microbeads, which make me look good but feel bad, and help me, O Lord, when I mislay my deepest dreams, to find a way to blame others that has resonance, even vaguely, as a trauma narrative.

(She thinks.)

And forgive me, Lord, for appropriating 'trauma.' It's just so *everywhere* at the moment. *(Her fingers flutter as though to indicate all the crazy trauma out there.)*

(She thinks.)

No offence, Lord. It's not Your fault.

(She thinks again.)

Well … it is and it isn't. Riiiight?

Anyway …

Stay safe!

Heartxoxheart,

Pochsy.

(Pochsy blows God a soft kiss. Her gloved fingers tremble. She sways a little, grips the mic.)

(Pochsy drags the heavy mic stand a few steps toward the audience. The dragging sound is very, very loud.)

Awkward Netflix Comedy Special

(Pochsy grabs the mic off the stand, and lights go super-stand-up bright. For a moment, she just gazes into the audience's eyes, like she has forgotten she is onstage. Then:)

How long has this been going on?

I'm not thirsty. I've had no new notifications. *(Beat.)* I do have a weird vaccine craving but it's not a desperate need, not yet, anyway …

(Little pause.)

I'm sorry about what I said earlier. About children. Some of them are very cute. My niece has a small child. Covid baby. Very bright. Her name is Malaaaaaria. Super-sweet. You just have to … reframe her.

(Pochsy strolls. The spotlight follows her. Regardless of how the audience responds over the following segment, Pochsy's delivery will parody all comedy stand-ups everywhere.)

How long *has* this been going on?

My niece just had another baby. 'Post-pandemic' baby born into 'Freeeedom!!!' *(She gently cries out an echo-y and diminishing 'freedomfreedomfreedom … ')*

I saw my niece's post, which featured the newborn itself in a little zebra onesie, and I hearted it, and I texted her, 'Cutest baby ever: what gender is it performing?'

(There may be a silence.)

My niece texted back, 'Got to go, baby's fussy.' So I texted, 'Well then. Female.'

(There is a silence.)

No text back. And I thought, riiiight, how binary I must seem. So I just called her!

In the background, I could hear the baby screaming maniacally. And I'm like, 'Okay then: male!'

(There may be another silence.)

But THEN the baby was giggling hysterically, and I realized: Oh. Wow. My niece's baby is Mad. How beautiful.

Christ himself has belatedly been diagnosed with a mood disorder. They found some of his DNA on, like, a goblet.

Or … thorn …

(feebly) Loin cloth …

(Pause. Pochsy scratches the grid on her mic. It's loud. She seems awkward in her body.)

Little Short Song

Sooooo, right about now, I should probably issue a content warning. Maybe should have done that sooner.

Anyway.

Please consider that if you remain in this room after this next song, your consent is implicit. You are clicking 'I agree.'

Five, six, seven, eight!

(Music in: upbeat Looney Tunes. Pochsy sings.)

This is a little short song,
Little short song,
This is a tiny song-gah!

(The tiny song ends abruptly. Pochsy squints into the audience to see if anyone is leaving.)

'Kay! So we're good!

(She takes the mic and flips the cord.)

So. What else is going on?

(Pochsy strolls.)

Awkward Netflix Comedy Special V2

Onstage, everything's glowing now, Netflix-style: walls are bright. Lit from below.

(softly) What else …

Oh! *(She smacks her forehead.)* I won a cruise!!!

Like, you know when someone calls you on your actual phone and they tell you you've won a cruise? Well, sometimes … you've actually won a cruise!

So I bought a bathing suit. Feministic bathing suit. Cuts my hyper-female flesh. Makes me look good but hate men. *(She winks at all the men in the room.)*

(She strolls. Tosses her mic between hands. Rifles through her internal apps.)

As well, I've been keeping it off the socials 'of late.' And prioritizing joy. Which, I mostly just try to have a beautiful feeling about the world, and to project that feeling out. Shine love in all directions. Which I believe is our ultimate purpose in this life …

Buuuuut …

(Pochsy gets a little conspiratorial.)

I was recently talking to a friend … IRL … *(she giggles)*.

(She strolls right up to the front row, maybe sits down beside someone.)

And when I say 'friend,' I do mean the kind of friend who, when you see her, she always asks, 'So how are you *doing*? *(Pochsy tilts her head, mimicking the friend)* You *okay*?'

In a way that makes you feel like you must not *seem* 'okay.'

So you just say, 'Hm! Nice boots!'And you talk about Big Tech, and benzos vs. Vyvanse, and laboratory meat, and Tesla door handles and the ethics around rescue dogs, plus the potential of sea grass foliage to save all life on earth …

But your friend is still there just staring at you like …

(Pochsy tilts her head again, imitating the friend:)

'You *okay?*'

(Beat.)

That kind of friend.

Anyway.

Since Mercury Packers, we've 'lost touch,' my friend and I. Though I wish her well. Because I believe no one is the same person today they were yesterday. *(beat)* I believe in my friend's ability to transform her own past into something that could be contained in a tattoo. *(beat)* And no offence to tattoos. I have a tattoo. It's very subtle. It's a tattoo of my own flesh. Made me feel such pain at the time. Now it's like nothing and I need to go to the parlour again, need that zap. That infusion of me-coloured ink. I don't do it for the look. I do it for the feels. I do it so I don't forget my own bland lineage, which …

Pontiac

(Lights shift: deep concert vibe. Now we're in a seventies MDMA *pink.)*

Anyway …

This next song is dedicated to anyone who has ever had a difficult conversation with a friend about anything from conspiracy theories to Critical Race Theory to French pronouns to forced tipping to affordable rockets to the new definition of freedom to whether or not it's okay to ride wild animals …

And you've come away from the conversation feeling misunderstood by your friend and lonelier than you've ever been.

(Pochsy sets her mic in the stand. We're full-on concert bright.)

It's called 'I've got the "I've just had a difficult conversation with a friend about everything from conspiracy theories to Critical Race Theory to French pronouns to forced tipping to affordable rockets to the new definition of freedom to whether or not it's okay to ride wild animals … and I've come away from the conversation feeling misunderstood by my friend and lonelier than I've ever been" … blues.'

(Beat.)

Only it isn't blues.

(Beat.)

It's folk.

(Beat.)

And it goes something like this.

(Music in. Joni Mitchell chords, only on a circus accordion. Pochsy sings sincere.)

> It came out on a single breath,
> I see you nowhere now.
> Your eyes have vapourized as though you're
> Holier than WOW.
> So let me take your ghostly hand
> Across this heinous chasm.
> I super-love your manicure:
> Polished ectoplasm.

(Pochsy flutters her blue-green gloved fingers as though they're in a virtual soak tray.)

The trails we've blazed may all be lost.
The walls we push through won't be soft.
But insulation's candy floss so
Come into to my taxi car.
A Pontiac whose driver cares.
Let's do nothing, let's just ride.
It's candy-flossy pink inside.
An Uber to nowhere.

It came out as a kind of wish,
I didn't guess the end.
But friends of Casper they all know:
Casper has no friends.

So ride in my electric car.
Windows down, we'll feel the air.
Let's do nothing, let's just ride.
It's candy-flossy pink inside.
An Uber to nowhere.

(She speaks over the music:)

And when I say 'nowhere,' I spell it with a 'k.'
'Know– *(she points to her head)* where…'

(She sings:)

It came out on a single breath,
And now you've flown from me.

I would say your eyes are pretty,
But they're – so hard to seeeeeeeeeeeee …

(The song ends, but Pochsy continues the 'seeeeeeeeee' into a kind of zombie vocal grill. For quite a while. Then:)

That song was inspired by my friend at work who shall remain anonymous.

But whose name rhymes with … Quelizabeth.

Quelizabeth in Quaccounting.

Quelizabeth with the rescue dog, the one she got during lockdown but was allowed to bring to work because, apparently, compared to handling dangerous chemical compounds, quaccounting can be soooo questressful.

(Pochsy is very regulated. She smooths her perfect hair.)

Speaking of money, as for the Joni Mitchell tune, she is no longer on Spotify, so I think it's cool.

(Pause.)

Also, Joni and I have very different vocal takes.

(Pause. Pochsy scratches her mic, absently. It's really, really loud. End of concert lights.)

Excuse me.

Fucking Patriarchy

(Pochsy crosses the stage. Absently pats her miniature bear knapsack, which is still high-profile in its mini-spotlight, and reaches into a first-aid kit. She carefully unboxes an aluminum bottle of water. She presents it to the audience, tilts it up to the light. She tries to open it. She can't open it. As with the gummy pack, she reeeeally tries. She fails. Exasperated, she storms back to centre. Crowds the mic.)

Um ... is there a strong cis-gender male in the house? Don't worry, we will not criticize you, I just need your help for a sec.

(House lights come up. There is awkwardness. With the audience's encouragement, or as a result of her flirtatious hypnosis, a strong cis-gender male comes to the main stage. Pochsy hands him the water bottle. As their hands touch, 'Theme from A Summer Place' plays over the PA: gritty, sentimental, old time-y. The cis-gender male easily opens the bottle and returns to his seat. Pochsy encourages applause for him. She drinks the entire bottle of water, then says, softly, flirtatiously:)

Fucking patriarchy... *(wink).*

(There is a moment between them. Then, to the audience:)

So, full disclosure, that last awkward little scene was written in partnership with AI. Prompts were: kindness, redeemable aluminum, and um ... *(she darts a glance at the dude and finds an appropriate phrase, like maybe 'George Clooney look-alike.')*

(She glances longer, more lingering.)

Anyway, sir, don't worry: you and I could never 'get together' as I myself am a neo-revolutionary foundationalist. And so we would not vibe.

(She flirts, nonetheless. Then:)

There are a few AI sections in this show, so that y'all know. Sometimes it's just …

(She taps her fingers on the mic.)

Faster.

(House lights fade to black. She snaps the mic cord.)

So … what else is going on?

Little Bird

(She drags the mic stand closer to the audience. Undeniable noise. Spotlight is cooler. Her face seems whiter.)

So, the day I won the cruise, it was …

Out of the blue, in the middle of the day, on an ordinary day.

(She smooths her hair. She smooths the mic.)

I was feeling a bit discombobulated – I dunno, I'd had like seven energy drinks, plus I had recently switched over to a new Sephora Rewards program, and as well I had just received that *(venomous)* fucking letter –

(She points. The crushed Mercury Packers letter seems to flare in its light. Then:)

I was in my house – which, by the way, is not my house, I just rent a tiny room, along with three roommates, but the kind of roommates you don't really know their last names, just we all worked at Mercury Packers, but on different shifts, unpredictable shifts, which had the effect of stealing our sleep, deranging our personal lives, as well as precluding the possibility of friendships with each other and …

I was on the phone, just giving the cruise agent my details – my address, my email, my banking information, my Social Insurance Number … mother's maiden name … lab results …

(She stops. Breathes for calm.)

But just as I was getting my confirmation number …

(Very soft) A little bird crashed into the front window of my house and died instantly. Fell to the front porch.

(Little pause.)

I looked that up.

Apparently, a bird falling in death on your front porch signifies a great change. Which, I'm like, maybe that change means death.

But then I thought … maybe this is not about me, but rather about my roommates!

Or maybe for me, *(little Chiclet grin)* it just means a cruise!

But just as I thought that …

(Softer) A second little bird flew into the window and fell onto the porch. This one did not die as immediately: a tiny pool of blood formed below its mouth – its … *(she corrects herself)* its *beak*.

I looked up its species. Which was … 'bird.' And apparently, certain birds eat certain berries which, when winter comes very late, can ferment on the branches and make little birds drunk. Make them fly into your window. Make unreal skies look real.

But just as I was googling 'how late must winter fall to count as "very late"?' I heard a crack. Sure enough, it was another bird. This one struggling to get back up.

It stepped very … *(she reaches for the word) intentionally* … down the front path. And laid its body down in the grass. So I went out to see it. To speak to it. To blow air into its little nose – its … *(she corrects herself)* its *beak*.

I held its little paw –

Its … *(brief doubt, then nodding, certain:)*

(soft) Its paw.

(Soundscape in: distant, sweet, like Looney Tunes backward birds.)

There are windows being made now that contain, within their glass, strands of the silk that spiders spin when they make their webs, and which birds can see, even when that substance is invisible to us.

I told the little bird to please hang on. Soon, I'm sure, the Green Corporations that are weaving that spider silk into their bird-protection glass will create a window economy wherein homeowners can buy those windows at consumer-friendly prices, and I promised the bird I would talk to my landlord, because they say that hearing is the last thing to go. When we pass. Which I think 'we' includes birds.

(Pause. Pochsy cups the mic in her hands. She's super close to it.)

I stroked the bird's feathers. I touched the tips of its little wings. I noted the intricate patterns in yellow and grey. The smooth symmetry of its nose. Its eyes were all pupil now, and it was as if I could see in them a miniature movie of all it had seen, all that it should have seen, and I could feel its tiny heart still beating in its plump little chest. Then I realized no, that's the pulse in my own thumb that I'm feeling. The little bird was dead. But in no way less magical for having died, because that too seemed like magic: the vanishing. The complication of its body, the bone of its beak, the … the *paws* were a bit … *(she cannot find words for the weirdness of the little bird's paws)* but still …

(She breathes deeply, unselfconsciously, into the mic.)

I let its little claws nearly pierce my fingers.
I observed those intricate patterns.
Exquisite yellow wing tips.
Upper tail coverts.
Sheeny belly.
Glowing scapulars.
Striped throat …
And I thought wow,
So complicated and beautiful.

(Pause.)

Like my iPhone.

(Beat. Another beat.)

Like my iPhone.

(There is a long silence as Pochsy contemplates the parallels between the little bird and her device. She twists the mic in its cradle, and it feeds back.)

Hmmmm. Hmmmmm …

(Pochsy runs her nails over the microphone's grid.)

(She just stares into the audience's eyes for a moment. Then she wanders. She leaves her mic and circles the stage. After a time, she drags her mic stand over to the white chaise and perches on the edge of it, beside her little leather bear. Dangling her heavy work boots daintily. By her feet, the crushed letter from Mercury Packers is aglow. She stares down at it.)

Sephora

(At the chaise.)

At Mercury Packers, they switched a few years ago, and we were all considered self-employed. Private contractors to Mercury Packers. It worked better for me 'cuz it gave me a little more wiggle room on my taxes, and it worked better for them because … it worked better for them.

But …

Soon after the transition process was the disaster. And soon after the disaster, I was in the company infirmary. And soon after that …

I opened my eyes.

I was all hooked up.

And there on the chair beside me was the Company Doctor.

(Pochsy flicks her hair, flutters her lashes. She pushes her bear aside and stretches out across the chaise. She removes her nitrile gloves very slowly, over the following.)

Dr. Doctor asked me a whole bunch of questions he had to get answers to put down on this form he was filling in. He asked me about the pressure gauges, and the filaments … He asked about the switches and the spill kits. Then he asked me about the disaaaaaster. And I'm, like, *(rolling her eyes)* I guess *that's* what this is all about.

So, he asked me: Back when I worked in shipping, did I ever handle the mercury with my hands?

I said: 'Well, doctor, if I had gloves on, then I wouldn't. But if I didn't … *(kittenish)* then I would.'

(She drops her doffed gloves.)

And besides. When you spill the mercury and it falls on the floor and bursts apart into all those shiny, sparkly little bubbles … ?

(Memory-sound of scattering mercury beads, like from an industrial Streetcar Named Desire.*)*

The best way to pick it up is to go like …

(She licks the tip of her naked finger, then mimes picking up a mercury bead with it.)

… that.

(Long pause.)

He stared at me intently. So I stared right back at him and I whispered,

(whispering) 'Doctor.

'There is no pinkness coming from the blood behind my skin.

(conspira-flirty) 'Do you have anything for that?'

Then he scribbles something in his freaky doctor handwriting, unplugs me from my needles and tubes … and I leave that infirmary with a cryptic reference letter, two weeks' pay, and a swag bag featuring a Mercury Packers water bottle, a 'Commitment to the Ideal' ball cap, and a twenty-dollar Sephora gift card for like … *anything!*

(Pochsy stares into space.)

I don't remember much after that.

(Pochsy stares into deeper space.)

I don't even remember driving home.

Soft Plastic

(Pochsy rises from the white chaise. Gently sets her little leather bear back in its spot. Lightly kicks her doffed nitrile gloves over to beside the crushed Mercury Packers letter. She goes to the first-aid kits. She pulls out a small square package. She takes it to the mic. Performs ASMR*: super-amplification as she almost fetishistically peels off the soft plastic wrapping, shows the audience the shiny cardboard box, and unboxes a plastic compact. She opens the compact and we hear the sound of hard plastic smacking.)*

Niiice ...

(Applying the blush with her bare fingers.) Starts off as a gel, but when you build it out it can give the illusion of a fresher face, like as if you just woke up, *(giggles)* only more put-together. Whether you're aiming for an afternoon at the gym – or a bold statement for ... *(she gestures out, indicating the audience)* an elegant evening event.

(Right beside the mic, she snaps the compact closed. She tilts her face up for the audience.)

Is that about right?

(Beat.)

Oh, I know, what's right, right? Depends on your body type ...

(Flicker of confusion.)

(She unzips her little bear's back and tucks the compact inside. Reaches in and feigns surprise as she pulls out a fresh pair of nitrile gloves.)

Oooh!

(Big Chiclet smile.)

I'm addicted!

(Pochsy zips her bear back up, sets him right, and wiggles her hands into her fresh gloves.)

(Almost to herself). So, so, so, so, so … What else … ?

(She snaps the gloves at her wrists. Steps to centre with her mic. Very still.)

If you want to know what you were doing in the past, look at your body now. But if you want to know what will happen to you in the future, look at what your mind is doing now.

(Music in: anthemic.)

I believe that I am led not by my fears, but rather by my dreams.

I believe that I make money, and that my work is valued.

I believe that I do not shoplift cheese. *(little smile)* Anymore.

I believe the future is now. It just hasn't happened yet.

And so I pray:

(Lights: vivid prayer state, like the previous kaleidoscope prayer, only more shimmering, Psilocybin-esque. Pochsy clasps her hands.)

Dear Lord:

Please give me courage and strength on this day. In this *world*. This world, which is a frightening place – no offence.

(Music in: delicate, music box.)

I just need to feel your love, my God, and to hear your song. Sing me your song of eternal love, and I will sing thy praises.

> Your love is heaven-sent, my Lord,
> Good God, it's raining love so true,
> I'd swear it on the graves below,
> What I don't know is what to do.

And I don't mean to criticize You, You're in a really tough spot these days – and also, backtracking a bit, to be clear, when I say 'eternal love' I do not mean eternal in the annoying sense, as in persisting tediously; I mean more 'eternality' or 'infinitude.' The universal spirit, which is sometimes super mysterious. *(she giggles, teasing)* If not completely baffling.

And perhaps even accidental *(she arches a brow)* … ?

> I worry 'bout the polar bears,
> I fear the bright red rocket glares,
> But Daddy, when I can't see you,
> What I don't know is what to do.

Whoa, sorry; *(she corrects herself)* 'Father.' But I think you know what I mean. *(Teasing again:)* Daddy.

Anyway, thanks for your time. My Lord. I know it's infinite, but … thanks anyway.

Love, Pochsy. xoxoxo

(Pochsy blows God a soft, sensuous kiss. Her fingers tremble like they are not fully attached to the palm of her hand.

Lights return to 'normal': stand-up comedy state, only more disorienting now. Light from the sides and footlights make Pochsy seem to be floating and bleach out her face a little.)

Swiping

So … so what else is going on?

(Pochsy swings the mic. She scratches it; the sound reverberates like some horror effect.)

(Then, brightly:)

So, my cruise had a *dating* app. A kind of dating app where you ask people questions so you don't waste precious time on the boat having destabilizing interactions and awkward experiments … IRL.

(Checks with the audience that she got that right. Tosses her hair.)

But the night before Sail-Away Day, I was on the dating app, and it wasn't working. The images were blurred. I could see names but they were just whizzing by. Until at one point, this one image came clear.

This … being.

There was no name. But though it was transparent, I could see it. It seemed to emerge from my phone. It seemed to step out.

(Lights spiral softly. We're in a kind of Romper Room spell.)

And when I say 'it' I say it because I simply can't tell what this being is. It exhibited only the absences of identities. Spectral opposites of what? Male? Female? Nonbinary? Alive? Dead? Undead? Non-living? Identifying as non-living? Both dead and alive? In a death confirmation moment? Or conjuring an illusion of life from a place of death?

In its eyes I saw the holy criss-cross of existence: the spectral stations of Life. Death. Animal. Mineral. Manufacturers. Consumers. And in its eyes, luminous, liquid, half-alive, living bodies, dying bodies, little babies being born.

The being was magnificent. Hovering. It wore a splendid hoodie, which it unzipped to reveal an *awesome* T-shirt.

It seemed to touch my face and it said,

(She speaks in its voice: echo-y.) 'Ask me anything.'

So I said, *(shy)* 'Okay … '

(Pochsy concentrates. She asks:)

'If you had to pick one, which would you rather *own*: a Labradoodle with a bit of a temper, or a pit bull who is super chill?'

(Suspenseful pause.)

It said, 'I would choose the Labradoo.'

I said, 'Me too.
'Now you do one.'

(She looks into where its eyes would be: she's back in time.)

It said, 'Okay. Which would you rather: live a long time moderately happy … or live a shorter time, wildly happy?'

(Pause.)

And I said: *(softly)* 'Well, that's easy.
(beat) 'Ask me another.'

It said, 'Okay then …
'Which would you rather *be*: lonely or frightened?'

(Long pause. Pochsy just stares at the being in her mind.)

And I said, *(super-soft)* 'That's too hard.'

(Longer pause.)

And then it said unto me, it said, 'What would it take for someone like me to get someone like you off this app?'

So I said, 'All you have to do is make me laugh.'

And it said, 'Okay:
'We live in a dream. We work and travel and eat and sleep … and we repeat these things as though they will never end.'

(Pochsy looks into the imaginary being's imaginary eyes. She laughs.)

And I laughed, and I laughed …

And it said,

(echo-y) 'Okay then. I am who you'll be wanting. I'll see you on the boat.'

And like a friend, it walked me down to the water's edge.

And like a ghost, it disappeared and sparkled off in all directions.

(Birds. Lights. Foghorn. Waves. Total transformation onstage. Lights are from all sides now and Pochsy appears suspended. There is sea mist.)

Sail-Away Day

And then.

A boat the size and shape of a whale pulled up to the dock. A seventeen-storey whale that glowed from within. It opened its colossal mouth. I walked across its grippy tongue … and took an escalator going down, down, down.

(Foghorn. Pink-red light bathes the stage.)

Imagine entering a lobby where the interior design is influenced by the connective emotional grid of social media platforms and virtual spaces where billions of people have learned to see and feel and want the same things. This boat was the S.S. Want. Need. Now. This boat was fuelled by the infinite power of unfolding possibility.™

(Deeper foghorn.)

Belly of the Whale

(Now, more intimate with the mic, Pochsy leans in like she's in court.)

In the belly of the whale, mammoth bones soared over the atrium and passengers murmured their delight at the light that bled through from the sky. The voices of little children echoed everywhere ... but it was very nice anyway.

I took a shot from a tray that came round, a little blue shot in a tiny perfect shot glass. A little glowing shot of blue that felt like warm snow inside my stomach. Until the snow melted and I wanted another.

I gave the shot four stars.

I ate a scallop from a toothpick that filled a scallop-shaped hole inside of me – except for where the toothpick had been. If I could have given that scallop five stars, I would have. But there was a tiny toothpick-shaped hole at the centre of the scallop that let the darkness in.

I gave the concierge desk four and a half stars: the concierges whose bodies I seemed to control by tipping, or ... *(coy)* by the promise of tips.

(For the rest of the cruise, Pochsy's spotlight will meld with magical cruise states: morphing night skies, turquoise water effects, stars. Strong side lights like on a boat will make it really dreamy. Floaty. Liquor-Disney.)

Beautiful Cruise

It was a beautiful cruise.

Famous for its path aside an underwater river that meant the currents flowed both ways: sea to sparkling river, river to sparkling sea. And on that first night, as night fell, the water was teeming with creatures from both: North Carolina Mountain Minnows and Bora Bora GloFish Sharks leapt and crisscrossed high above the boat's glimmering wake.

A deer swam beside us for a while. It wanted on. Its antlers were grand: a seven-year-old. Majestic. And, after a while, a little sea otter climbed onto the deer's back … and they both disappeared as the wake flared and foamed and spray dimmed the light from the sky.

(In her mind, Pochsy goes to the deck rail and looks out over the water. Music pads sneak in steadily: moody, watery, underwatery …)

My heart had grown heavy and my mind had grown dull with … overwhelm. I had become passive and disoriented.

But then, I don't know if it was the sparkles on the water, or the dappled twilight sky – or the unlimited mojito tap – but on that night, it was as though I could hear a voice say, 'It's okay, Pochsy. Everything's going to be okay.'

It was a beautiful cruise.

(Now she will actually walk into the audience. Light will go with her. She will look into people's eyes, enchanted. She will often speak to individuals in the house, as though she is losing any self-consciousness around space, her body. She may drag her mic along a railing or the backs of chairs. Loudly. She is not even conscious of it.)

Tendons

(Intimate with an audience member.)

Look at me. Please look at my hand. *(She extends her gloved hand.)*

I see my hand, its tendons and veins, and I know that it is made up of billions of atoms that came from the belly of a star that came from the belly of a star that came from a belly of a star that came from the belly of a star… Some of these atoms might be atoms from Napoleon's body, or Cleopatra's, or, like …*(indicating another audience member)* someone more normal … *(she smiles reassuringly at them)*.

But I mean … *(she looks at another person's hand, gets very close)* how do these atoms know how to be? How molecules must be to make water? Or a hand?

(Very soft) Or a paw?

(She holds very still.)

It was a beautiful cruise …

Rescue Dogs

Part of its thing was a mindfulness around lost and neglected animals in the impoverished villages on the little islands the boat would pass through, scooping up street dogs and finding more North American homes for them. More 'I'll rescue you, you rescue me' homes.

(She drifts back to the stage. Turquoise water reflects and ripples across her body.)

I had gone to the Rescue Dogs App before we embarked: gave my email, my mail-mail, my banking information, Social Insurance Number, mother's maiden name …

And so I was invited on a day trip to one of those islands where I got a tour of a green seagrass foliage farm that local children had built in a plan to save all life on earth, and I got, as well, a mani-pedi.

(She flutters her gloved fingers.)

I went to where they were selling seashells. By the seashore. But they were fresh out. So I dove into the water, where I found some nestled in a cheerful tangle of kombu and tinsel. I pulled out the prettiest *(demonstrates, like an unboxing)*, pried it apart with my brand-new French tips, plucked out the little sea creature … and let it swim free.

(Pochsy's fingers trace the creature's path. Sound: sonic swimming sea creature.)

It was a beautiful cruise.

(She looks into audience eyes. Stand-up-comedy-strolls like before, only as the story sails, she's looking a bit chalkier.)

(Soft) What else, what else, what else …

On the fourth day of my cruise, I took a TikTok dance class *(she demonstrates briefly)*.

On the sixth day, I saw a show. Trigger warnings were Spandex, Nestle water, and Toxic Positivity.

On the seventh day of my cruise, I heard the rescue dogs being taken into quarantine.

(Beat. She holds very still.)

Excuse me.

Aromatherapy

(Pochsy crosses to the first-aid kits. Opens the smallest and pulls out a tiny box. She unboxes it. Inside, there is a tiny glass vial. Pochsy sniffs it like a drug.)

Don't worry, it's nothing weird. Just a little aromatherapy. It's for … *(she reads the label)* 'feeling destabilized by the escalating back-and-forth between one's own physical and digital evolution.'

(She performs a little ASMR into the mic: soft rubber stopper on glass. It doesn't make much noise. Pochsy doesn't seem to care.)

Where was I … ?

(Lights dim around her. Now the sound of water rushing is more present. Otherworldly lights glow swimming-pool blue and it is as if the light is from below, from underwater cabins. Or GloFish. In the blue light, Pochsy seems whiter still.)

Stars Stars Stars

It was a beautiful cruise.

Every evening, in the evening, the glittering creatures from the water would skitter across the deck, and the stewards would throw them back into the sea, and they'd skitter back, *(giggling)* and all the little children would watch, laughing and squealing … and hanging onto the deck rails for dear life.

Every evening, in the evening, the stars would come out one by one, and the further out to sea we sailed, the more planets and stars we could see:

The Big Dipper …
The glorious Milky Way …
The planet formerly known as Pluto …

Every night, the Northern Lights would come on and it was as though I could reach out and touch them.

I gave the Northern Lights three stars.

I would have given them four stars, but some of the … *(she tries to name the arcs of light; the swirling rivers of atoms, nitrogen)* they were … *(her fingers describe electrons, molecules, neon light)* they were …

Indistinct.

Drinks and Dogs

On the eleventh day of my cruise, I ordered, through my drinks app, a Clamato cocktail with seven different liqueurs in it.

It was bespoke.
I invented it.
It was disgusting.
I sent it back.
I tipped no one.

If I remember correctly … It was then that I heard the dogs again. And I wondered which one was mine. Just as the sea began to roil and thunderheads appeared where the boat was heading.

(Foghorn. Now deeper. Birds and animals cry. There is weather.)

There's something weird about spending so many days on a boat.

(She wanders. She stills. She smooths her hair. Smooths the mic. There is a Very. Long. Pause. And then:)

On the thirty-seventh day of my cruise, I got an upgrade. I was upgraded to Premium Dining.

(Radical atmospheric shift to a Caesar's Steak House look and feel. Velvety.)

Upgrade

I was now dining with a billionaire in a hoodie, a single mother in an evening gown, a frontline health care worker on oxygen, a Ukrainian soldier with a guitar, a teen-America skinfluencer, and the ship's star lecturer, a sexy Climate Scientologist. They were the entertainment.

There was also a very tiny child, whose lecture topic was *(a little brittle)* 'Robot Rights.'

It was difficult when everyone expressed their opinion, but given that we were all from different walks of life, we did pretty good. Everyone started their sentences with 'Look.' And then, 'I think,' or 'I believe,' or 'There's a podcast you should,' and of course the ever-popular *'Well, maybe, buuuut …'*

One night, I was sitting next to the billionaire, who actually had Invisible Hands, which, if you do not know the term, is a metaphor for unseen forces at play in the economy, and I asked him what it feels like to have everything you do be touched by death, and also could I please have some money.

But just as he was about to answer, the very tiny child started kicking the leg of my chair. I asked her to stop, but she seemed somehow unable to. So after a while, when she got up to go to the bathroom, I waited for a minute … and then I followed her.

I went to where she was standing in line, in her little sundress, with her little pink legs sticking out the bottom … *(careful, like in court:)* And I kicked her in the back. *(Palliating:)* Very gently.

I explained everything to her. How irritating it was …

I suggested she needed to learn empathy. To think of others. To think of all the people who will never go on a cruise. Hungry children who don't even know what a buffet IS. What a chocolate waterfall IS. All the future people – trillions of generations who may never even get to EXIST … depending on how things go.

(The Caesar's Steak House red glows redder. Pochsy speaks to the tiny child in her mind.)

I said, *(gently)* 'You might want to start *now* to think about where best to place your energies. What *you* can do to generally make the world saner. To think about perhaps not the *length* of civilization, but rather the *quality* of civilization that could fly in the face of bio weapons, species loss … and capture the enormous potential of the future – which conceivably lies in your tiny, glowing hands.

'The opposite of civilization's collapse.'

(Pochsy thinks. Or remembers thinking.)

She thought about that, very hard. Furrowed her little brow. And after a moment or two, she asked me if … before she was born … if I had ever thought of *her*.

I thought about that.

(She thinks again.)

And I said no.

And then I realized this child may not be very bright.

I said, 'Okay then. Sleepy time. Close your eyes and imagine if where your head is now … there was nothing. If on this voyage, surrounded by glittering water and powdery stars and Mountain Minnows leaping and GloFish sneaking by … that all you are is them. You are beyond fear. Beyond dread. Because you are a child of the stars. And everything is exactly as it should be.

'The universe is a powerful force, little girl.

'The universe will protect you.'

And after a moment or two, the little girl said *(imitating the adults at the table)*,

'Well, maybe, buuuuut …'

(There is a pause.)

Just then, I received a notification *(there is a ping)*: I had been awarded a cabin upgrade. I went to my new cabin. It was a balcony cabin. The balcony looked into the lobby.

(Pochsy walks, a bit oddly. She leans into a rail.)

I received another notification *(ping)*: it was my dating app. But there was no spectral message there.

(Now orange smoke creeps onto the edges of the floor. This is the orange nautical smoke that signals distress on a boat. It rolls out slowly.)

Then came a page over the deck speakers. *(ping ping ping)* They had matched me with a dog.

The steward walked me to the kennel deck. I heard the dogs barking: a Labradoo, a pit-bull-poo, and a miniature … something.

I wondered which one was mine.

(Pause.)

But what I saw when I stepped inside the kennel was a dog that was all three.

It was a three-headed dog.

There were snake heads growing out of its back, and it had seven serpents' tails, which it wagged and wagged, so happy it was to meet its new owner.

It will need extra food, they told me. They said it had generalized anxiety disorder. ADHD. PTSD. It might have behavioural issues and fight with its own heads. Heart condition.

I patted the dog's complicated fur. I taught it to shake a paw. I gave it a cookie, a cookie … then another cookie. I kissed each of its three foreheads.

Then, as they took my dog back to quarantine, I looked into its … various eyes … and I said,

'I'll rescue you if you rescue me.'

(Pochsy swoons a little. Ship lights and orange smoke transform her: her skin seems nearly grey.)

Makeover

(Pochsy speaks the following in tandem with a recorded voice-over. It's distorted, amplified, crunchy like in an old movie theatre.)

POCHSY (IN VOICEOVER): Day 68. There is a storm. A terrible storm. A hurrinaaaado. They say that eating can mitigate seasickness, but passengers are on the deck, leaning over the rail, coughing up whole all the little animals they have eaten. Baby calamari squirm across their tongues and plumped mussels and Arctic char fall from their mouths and swim away. Whole.

Having taken some black-market antidote for seasickness, I wander through the lower-level shopping mall. It is night-time even though it is daytime.

(Pochsy tries to stroll with elegance, but it's a dead-girl walk: her body is all wrong.)

In the Duty Free, the L'Occitane smells like gasoline. I complain to the Sephora cosmetologist that I don't have any pinkness coming from the blood behind my skin. She gives me a makeover that just slides off my face.

(Pochsy goes to the first-aid kits and unboxes a raincoat. It is bright pink, matching her blush, and it is shimmery.)

I walk among the others. And I wonder how many people are on this boat? How many are there supposed to be?

(She dons the shimmery coat. Does a perfunctory 'fit check.)

I go back up to the deck. Not sure where my phone is. Not sure if that's a problem. But it's a fucking problem. And so I say,

'Dear Lord.

'Dear Lord.

'Dear Lord …'

(She returns to mic and grips the stand.)

(A whisper.) 'Could you please call my phone?'

(Everything falls away into shadow now except Pochsy. Her pink raincoat is wet, and it blazes in the light.)

Sailing With God

And then. He is with me.

I don't recognize God at first. Because, as with many celebrities, he looks different in the flesh. Just looks like some Hollywood star: slouchy sexy jeans, seven-day stubble … and a splendid hoodie, which he unzips to reveal an *awesome* T-shirt.

The T-shirt has graphics, which I can't read because they are in an ancient religious language that I have never spoken.

We lean against the railing, me and God, and look out over the water rushing by. Glittering animals are clinging to the boat. Some are speeding away.

We sail past craters and mudslides and forests and poppy fields and entire cities built into walls with cafes and casinos and babies and teenagers with flesh grown over their devices.

Bombs. Drones. Roiling water.

A baby Mountain Minnow leaps onto the deck and lies there, panting. Exhausted, I suppose, from its fight against the undertow. I lift it into my lap and stroke its tiny fins … then I rock it in my arms until it falls to sleep.

(Pause.)

I confess to God that sometimes I do get him mixed up with Christ. And I notice that his T-shirt has transformed. It now sports a picture of His Son.

So cute, I think, God has a picture of His Son on his T-shirt.

The tide pulls away and we are on a sandbar.

We talk about this and that … all the future people … He tells me which stocks to invest in and that neo-banking is bullshit.

He returns often to the question of 'the future people.' The existential risk of an endless dystopia. His long-term guess for humanity.

I say, 'Guess?'

I look into the eyes of God and I ask him *(head tilted, imitating Quelizabeth)*, 'Are you *okay?*'

He says,

'I've been better.'

The ocean pulls away and we are in the desert. The clouds part and the Northern Lights come on. God doesn't even look at them.

I ask him what I can do. 'The world is in disarray, I am perpetrator, I know, paralyzed by the things I have done, or not done. Guilty from the night that I was born. I barely remember my family, I am a pink-brand feminist, a kitchen environmentalist. I am terrified of my friends: we are all like bones that have fractured and are trying to grow back together inside one body that is Yours. *(desperate)* What can I do, my Lord? How can I save this?

'Yes, I have heard of effective altruism.

'Yes, I have heard of conscious selflessness.

'And yet nothing seems to get traction.'

'WHAT AM I MISSING?

'MY LORD!'

Then God points to his T-shirt, which has transformed yet again. And now it says …

(Softly.)

'Well, this dick isn't going to suck itself.'

(Beat.)

(Beat.)

(Pochsy's jaw drops, delicately.)

And I know that he's joking. Jest of God, riiiight? You have to have a sense of humour in times like these.

(Pochsy looks deep into the eyes of the audience.)

And God wraps his arm around me from behind, so that his forearm spreads and looks bigger than it actually is. And he whispers in my ear, 'Hail Pochsy, full of grace. Blessed be thy wounded body. Blessed be thy wounded mind.'

I look up and I see Orion's Belt.

I give Orion's Belt five stars.

It is simple and clear.

Soft Grey Coils

(Atmospheric waves swim across the stage: electrons and neon light.)

And I am soaring. Transcending. Walking across God's slippery tongue and flying down his silvery esophagus into the sea inside him where I can see all our bones glowing in an ultrasound ocean. All our little organs lit bright. Minerals reaching across cavities toward each other, our collagen luminous from accidents and spa treatments.

His intestines are infinite and wallpapered with that green sea foliage.

I lie down in the soft green and I can breathe in it like I am not underwater at all.

But I am hurled by a spasm up into the soft grey coils of the brain of God: unending velvet dark.

And from inside the brain of God I see a little bird. Perched on the far shore.

I see the far shore.

(Foghorn.)

(Very. Long. Pause.)

(We are in a new state now. Like the end of Wizard of Oz. *We get there by going backwards through all the lighting states we've seen.)*

(Pochsy leaves her mic and walks. She walks and walks. At first she walks stiff and dead-girl-style. Then her body gets more silvery and frictionless. She returns to the centre of the stage. She tests her mic. She smooths her coat, her hair, her face.)

It was a beautiful cruise.

But there's something weird about spending so many days on a boat. So I was actually happy for disembarkation day. I was happy to get back home.

Now, every evening, in the evening, I watch the sun set down over ol' Mercury Packers and I ponder refraction and the physics of a lime-green sky.

Every evening, in the evening, I step inside the house that is not my house and climb up all the stairs. Every evening, I brush my teeth with fish-friendly tooth polish and apply an illuminating body serum that makes me feel like a candy-box goddess.

In my tiny room there is a bed. On the bed, my three-headed dog. And every evening, I give God my thanks for my animal, and tears fall from my eyes and onto the floor where they burst apart into a thousand shiny, sparkly bubbles.

(Pochsy tosses her hair and we hear tiny beads scatter.)

Every evening, I curl up beside my three-headed dog, and next to its warm body, my body is a dogbodydoggybodydoggygod-bodydoggybodydoggygod child from the belly of a star.

Every evening, I whisper soft nothings into my dog's numerous ears.

My 'I'll rescue you if you'll rescue me' dog.

(There is a bit of time.)

One Big Dreamy Whale

(Lights: brilliant. Like a prayer state from before, only this is white light. Stark and blazing: there is no colour coming from the blood behind Pochsy's cheeks.)

So, thank you all for coming along. *(Beat.)* Everybody.

This last song is inspired by those of you who have worked hard, played hard. By those who committed to the ideal when you didn't even know what that would even mean. Accidents will happen.

(Pochsy's blue-green fingers flutter delicately, and she looks up and out.)

This song is dedicated to Mercury Packers, and to the dying of its light.

Every morning in the morning,
I dreamed you.
Then I dreamed you dreamed of me.
You bathed me in your cathode light,

It happened
Happy accidentally.

In the stillness of the night,
I felt the pressure, then I felt the squeeze.
Touched a screen and saw the face of God,
Ground Control to Major Me.

And when your walls
Come tumbling down,
I'll be haunting you.
If that's okay.

And when your glass
Is all broken through,
I will still dream,
Dream of you.

(Music at full concert. Pochsy goes full-on Swift. Only more cadaver-like. Strides the front of the stage.)

So, what else is going on? What else … ? *What? What? What? What? What? Whaaaaat?*

(TikTok dance break: Pochsy reincorporates gestures from earlier in the show: freeing the sea creature, licking her finger and picking up mercury, prayer poses, fetishistic unboxing gestures … She dances and her pink raincoat shimmers wild.)

Milk and honey, I dreamed the dream,
And that was one big dreamy whale.
But you won't see me when you dream me next,

'Cuz I'll be
So see-through behind this veil.

And when the rain
Comes pummelling down,
I'll remember you,
If you remember me.
And when the sky
Comes tumbling down,
I'll dream of you,
If you dream of me,
Or who I dreamed I'd be.
Please, please dream
Who I dreamed I'd be.

So, thank you all for being here. Thank you for your time. I know it's not infinite.

(She winks.) Just kidding.

(She does a final twirling 'fit check: skirts, boots, brace, gloves.)

(Almost chanting:) Who am I? Who am I now? Who am I? Who am I now?

My name is Pochsy. Taxpayer. Working Girl.

(Pochsy TikTok dances and dances as light and vapour conjoin to obscure her glowing face. Her pink raincoat gleams out. She blows the audience a soft kiss, then fades into blackness.)

Finis.

Literary and Musical Acknowledgements

Marcus Aurelius, Sandra Balcovske, Blake Brooker, Kevin Brooker, Imajyn Cardinal, Jaydra Dawn, Roland Griffiths, Douglas Harding, Sam Harris, David Hines, Margot Hines, Maggie Huculak, Matthew Jocelyn, Michael Kennard, Kate Lynch, William MacAskill, Zoe McKeown, George Monbiot, Justin Miller, Joni Mitchell, Greg Morrison, Amy Rutherford, Sandi Somers, Michelle Thrush, Jia Tolentino, John Turner, Chantal Vitalis, Alana Wilcox, Cybèle Young.

Karen Hines is the author of *Crawlspace*, *All the Little Animals I Have Eaten*, *Drama: Pilot Episode*, *Hello... Hello (A Romantic Satire)*, and *The Pochsy Plays* – all published by Coach House Books. Her plays and productions have been presented internationally, and have won many production and literary nominations and awards including twice being finalist for the Governor General's Award for Drama and shortlisted for the 2020 Siminovitch Prize in Theatre. A Second City alumna, and an associate of One Yellow Rabbit Performance Theatre, Karen has also appeared in numerous television and film productions and is the award-winning director of cult horror clowns Mump & Smoot. Raised by scientists in Toronto, she now lives in Calgary.

Typeset in Granjon and Futura PT.

Printed at the Coach House on bpNichol Lane in Toronto, Ontario, on Zephyr Antique Laid paper, which was manufactured, acid-free, in Saint-Jérôme, Quebec, from second-growth forests. This book was printed with vegetable-based ink on a 1973 Heidelberg KORD offset litho press. Its pages were folded on a Baumfolder, gathered by hand, bound on a Sulby Auto-Minabinda, and trimmed on a Polar single-knife cutter.

Coach House is located in Toronto, which is on the traditional territory of many nations, including the Mississaugas of the Credit, the Anishnabeg, the Chippewa, the Haudenosaunee, and the Wendat peoples, and is now home to many diverse First Nations, Inuit, and Métis peoples. We acknowledge that Toronto is covered by Treaty 13 with the Mississaugas of the Credit. We are grateful to live and work on this land.

Edited by Alana Wilcox
Cover and interior design by Crystal Sikma
Cover photo by Gary Mulcahey
Author photo by Tim Leyes

Coach House Books
80 bpNichol Lane
Toronto ON M5S 3J4
Canada

mail@chbooks.com
www.chbooks.com